Foreword

In today's world where world travel by air to distant parts of the globe is so easy and accessible to almost everyone in the United Kingdom, the idea of sea power and what it means to an island race such as ours is slowly being lost and yet over 90% of what we eat, wear or consume in our manufacturing industries still come to us by sea. Lynn New, in her new book, 'Time and Tide' takes the reader back to times when sea power was the predominant thinking of a nation. When the majority of industry in the Portsmouth area was of a maritime nature, it's threads ran through the communities and into the lives of the poorest and the richest; from the harlots of the Hard to the solitary sentry manning the fortifications; from the fishmonger's daughter to the Dockyard matie. All were aware of its importance and the tragedy of treating the sea with contempt. Time and Tide is in essence a window to the past where the reader can peer into the lives of the people portrayed and the hardships they endured and the great events that stirred the hearts of those who set the stage for what we today called history.

It was many years ago now that Lynn New was ushered into my office in hope that I would relate some of the Portsmouth's Dockyard history so that she could put it into poetry for a set of cards to sell in No7 Boathouse. It was from this small beginning that her interest in Dockyard history developed, but as she quickly discovered you can not look at the history of the Dockyard without looking at the City of Portsmouth and the Royal Navy and the people who worked in these services and communities in which they lived. Her talent at creating poetic verse from historical events is not widely seen in the modern publishing world, which is a loss to those interested in history as it adds a dimension to the subject that is often inspiring and fun.

It is for this reason that I would recommend 'Time and Tide' for it's creative approach to the social, military and maritime history of those who live within the area of the Spithead Anchorage.

B.H.Patterson.
Curator & Keeper of Historic Boats
Portsmouth Naval Base Property Trust
30th March 2005

Acknowledgements

My thanks and gratitude go to Mr. Brian Patterson without whose help 'Time and Tide' would not have been conceived or completed. His support and patience in dealing with my many questions and detail confirmations have taken the book from the romantic to the historically correct and his enthusiasm for his subject has fired me in my own. If my book opens a window to history, then it is because he opened the door. I would also like to thank Peter Cross for his foresight and professional ability in getting 'Time and Tide' into print and Fiona Crouch for her technical ability and creative balance into producing its final format. Finally I would like to thank my friends for their patience and concern when it seemed I had dropped off 'the ends of the earth', so single minded has been the commitment to my latest book. Thank you all.

First Published in 2005 by
COLOUR- CREATE PUBLISHING
Les Chenes, Oakhill Road
Seaview, Isle of Wight

Printed by
MPG Books, Bodmin

ISBN 0 9550 493 0X

F.B.S.R.O.

Complement of Poems

This listing is not a full index. It serves as a catalogue of the poems included but within each selection I have included paragraphs of text relating to the era or the events depicted in the individual poetry.

Preface

'Time and Tide' was never intended to be written as a historical document, however from an encouraged seed my enthusiasm grew for the people whose lives were controlled by our maritime and military past. As the picture unfolded I became involved with their stories and have included a selection that will in time become our history. I hope the reader will share my fascination for the faces behind the facts.

Romancing History

It was miserable, cold, chilly and wet;
I struggled on my way home.
I thought of the warmth that awaited me;
The comfort I'd always known.
I was dreaming of all the images
As I pulled my coat to keep warm
And as I passed Old Sally Port
I felt the blast of the storm.

By a trick of the light and the sound of rain
I was suddenly made aware
Of a figure crouched low and sheltering;
I found it hard not to stare.
I made as if to acknowledge him,
Though was keen to be on my way.
I nodded in his direction but found
The man had nothing to say.

I quickened my step and left him behind,
Turning north and away from the sea,
But I couldn't forget that shadowy soul,
It was if he was following me.
His thoughts began to infiltrate mine,

Till I slowed down my pace to recall
Whether the figure had spoken to me,
Or whether I'd seen him at all.

He seemed to be saying, 'Know me or not,
It doesn't matter, you see.
You have a question for answering
And it seems that I hold the key.
You glanced, as you passed, at my pitiful form,
Intrigued and embarrassed to find
The more you tried to forget about me,
The more I came in to your mind.

You're questioning life, dear child, I fear
Without the wisdom of age.
Let history write each chapter in turn,
While people record every page.
My book may be closed, yet I will live on
While there are those who believe
In the balance of past and present as one
With future yet to conceive.

The old Sally Port, the embarkation gateway for innumerable sea journeys

Gunwharf Quay

Gunwharf to Gunwharf

Been shopping at Gunwharf; dead on your feet?
Sit down and relax on a waterfront seat.
Watch people pass, enjoying the view;
Ferries and yachts just passing through.
But do not forget that Gunwharf was famed,
Not for shop retail but why it's so named.
Its role was essential; munitions were stored;
Canon and rifle bullet and sword.
The Board of Ordnance then owned the right
To supply to the forces equipment on site.
Guns to the Crimea, torpedoes to sea,
Until in the year Nineteen twenty three
H.M.S. *Vernon* took over it all.
The establishment formed a new Training School.
Alas with the government change was about;
Cutbacks were made and the Navy lost out.
The site was sold on as real-estate land,
The Gunwharf project respectfully planned.
So when you have shopped and eaten, look round;
Up to the tower and down at the ground
And remember that history lies 'neath your feet,
For here past and present
Comfortably meet.

Naval Ordnance, H.M. Gunwharf

The *Royal George* ended her naval career in 1782, when she went down at Spithead after a tragic and avoidable accident. The loss of life was over eight hundred souls. Many were civilians who had gone aboard while she was at anchor and loading stores, therefore the exact total could not be tallied.

Portsmouth and Gosport were hard hit by the tragedy and those washed up on the Isle of Wight coast at Ryde were buried, only to be disturbed in 1840 by building development of that time.

In 1965 a new memorial to the loss of The *Royal George* was opened by Earl Mountbatten, on the same site, now known as East Esplanade. Their final resting place had been granted.

The next poem has been inspired by the tragic event.

The Loss of the Royal George

29th August 1782

Did God choose His moment, or the devil his way
That August at Spithead, where The *Royal George* lay?
She rested at anchor, a ship of the line,
Three days before sailing the weather held fine.
Her water-cock open to wash down the deck;
A problem discovered, a fault then to check.
Reports from The Dockyard, repairs to be made.
The ship must be heeled and on her side laid.
The order was given next day before eight;
Larboard guns run out to shift the ship's weight.
Her lower deck port cills at sea level held;
Repair work commenced as the sea gently swelled.
Now The *Lark* came alongside just before nine
And at the ship's larboard she secured a line.
Hands were then piped, 'Clear lighter,' the call
And her cargo of rum was unloaded by all.
The ship was remaining all on one side
But water was shipped as the wind caught the tide.
Men still slung their casks and hoisted their load.
The wind shifted further as cargo was stowed.
The carpenter stated the list had increased;
The lieutenant on watch cared not in the least.
Her angle alarming for weight and for wave
Had multiplied danger and risk of the grave.
The water was flooding the ports at each swell,
Soon none would escape the whirlpool of hell.
The drummer was called; the decision came late.
There was no, 'beat to quarters' to alter their fate.
They tumbled down hatchways and tried to correct
The list of their vessel with little effect.
She turned in a moment for ports open wide
Took the weight of the water through her larboard side.
The decks fell below the crew as they fought

To climb to the light which they franticly sought.
In the confusion some jumped and some tried,
While others encumbered, by drowning soon died.
Many were trapped, some fought to be free,
But The *Royal George* sank; she was claimed by the sea.
She gave up the ghost and sank on her side
Eventually setting her masts towards Ryde.

An enquiry stated hundreds were lost,
Dragged to the deep or in the tide tossed.
None could equate the final sad score,
For bodies were washed on each sheltered shore.
Some, landed at Ryde and are peacefully laid
Their final chapter eventually played.
She ended her reign as a danger to shipping
Blasted, destroyed, into memory slipping.

The Royal George going down at Spithead

Admiral Nelson

Let us remember Nelson
And conjure up his name
That speaks of brave tenacity,
Untimely death and fame.
The Battle of the Nile;
Trafalgar's victory,
An Admiral of time and place
And naval history.

Let us recall his life
And famed career;
Of battles fought and won,
Of life and death and fear.
But let us not forget
This legend was a man
Who lived and loved in full,
Though short his earthly span.

Let us rally now,
Not just to battle's cry.
Nor dwell too long on loss of limb,
Nor sightless eye.

Let us hold him up
As hero of the hour;
A man of diplomatic strength
And naval power.

Let us now salute
The valour of his day,
Remembering the past
And yet in present pray
His courage and charisma
Be born in man anew;
That every modern Englishman
May, 'Do his duty' too.

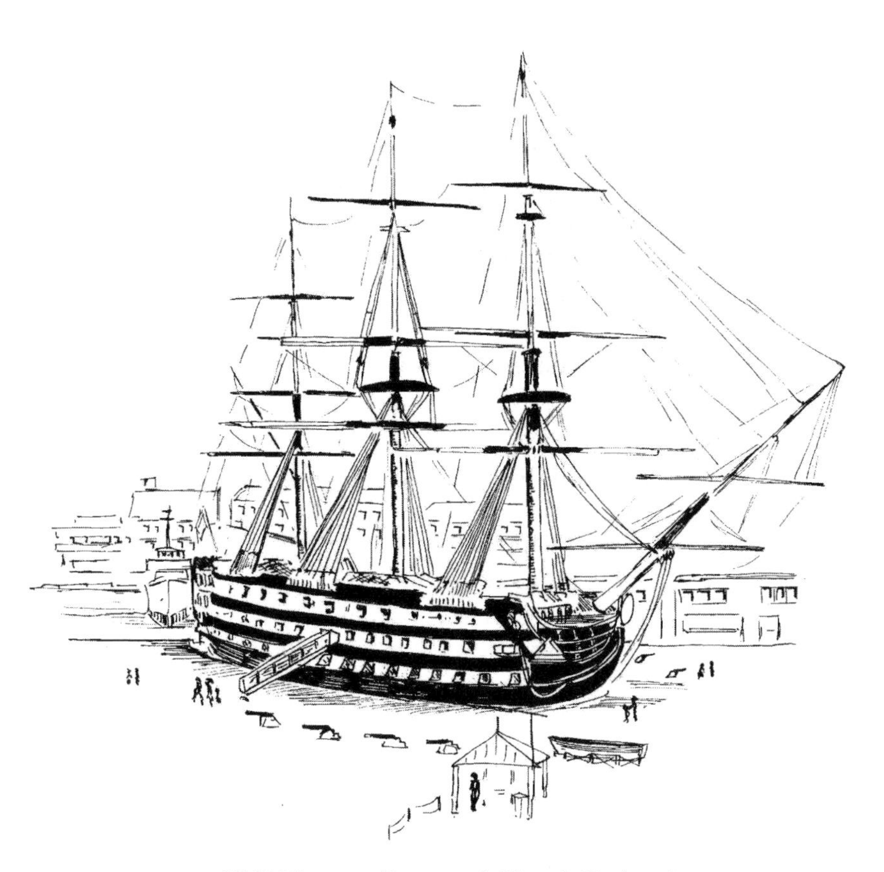

HMS Victory at Portsmouth Historic Dockyard

The Dreadnought Age. 1905-1920

The *Dreadnought* was an epoch making battleship, giving her name to all future ships of her class. She was built on the massive scale and proportion that was unrivalled throughout the world. In materials and work hours alone she could not be matched and the skilled and determined workforce laboured through many hours of overtime to see the *Dreadnought* join the British Battlefleet.

The celebrated launching in record time of these great ships brought a boost to the morale of the country and the British people. The poem gives an insight to the launching of the first of these great giants.

The Launching of the Dreadnought

10th February 1906

Bunting and garlands and pennants that fly,
Stages and gantries built to the sky.
Best hats and parasols, clean linen shirts,
Shoes for the mudlarks that squeeze till 'it hurts!'
People in thousands, by hundreds they've grown
To witness the birth of one like their own.
Proud folk and hard folk will soften today
When 'Rule Britannia' strikes up to play.
Out of the houses and thronging the street;
Jostling neighbours and workmates who meet
Each shift at the Dockyard though today is the day
They pay their respects and send her on her way.
Up on the staging fine feathers will fly;
No nearer to heaven, but nearer the sky.
Admirals and Ladies, directors and Lords
Look up at her grandeur and down at the hoards.

Oh such achievement, a vision in steel;
It wasn't so long since they laid down her keel.
Now she's a giant, she shadows the light;
Solid in shape; a magnificent sight.
Just as it seems the excitement will burst
A signal is given and a line well rehearsed
Is made by our King from where he is standing
And thousands of eyes look to the launch landing.
He swings out the bottle, the moment is now
And crowds cheer their hearts out; it breaks on her bow.
Now centuries of custom is then re enacted,
He's handed the launch box, the chisel's extracted.
He strikes with the mallet, the rope's sliced in two,
The weighted release then follows on through.
It knocks out the dog shores that hold her so tightly.
The ship is released; she's free and quite rightly.
Then just for a moment the tension's unbroken,

The Dockyard is hushed and no word is spoken.
It seems like an age, soon she's moving, she's free.
With gathered momentum she slips to the sea.
Now the crowds and the Ladies, the Lords and the chaps
Wave their white hankies and their flat caps.
Then gradually silence; the cheers fade away,
Home to their houses; the end of the day.
They will remember, those privileged few
What it was like to be granted the view
Of the launch in its glory, the prestige, the fame;
For the hearts of the people will bear *Dreadnought*'s name.

H.M.Y. Britannia returns to Portsmouth

The Royal Yacht served the Queen and the Royal family for forty three years until she retired from her illustrious career as floating ambassador in 1997. Her paying off ceremony was held in Portsmouth on 11th December of that year, attended by Queen Elizabeth. *Britannia* is now in residence at the port of Leith, under the protection of The Royal Yacht Britannia Trust and for the first time is open to the general public.

Much has been written about H.M.Y. *Britannia,* but to be on the water waiting for her final return to Portsmouth with thousands of enthusiastic supporters on shore and afloat, sums up the love and patriotism she inspired.

As the next poem recounts, I was lucky enough to be one of them.

The Royal Flotilla

Throbbing diesel engine, throaty so of voice,
Leaving now the harbour, leaving of her choice.
Chugging little motor, sister to them all,
Feeling the excitement, answering the call.
Sophisticated cruiser cutting water well.
She is one of many, meeting on the swell.
Single seated kayak, brave her captain be,
The joy of his conviction setting him to sea.
Ex-naval vessels answer a call within the heart,
Returned again to service, proud to take their part.
Renovated trawlers with week end workers keen
Jostle for position upon this royal scene.
The cry is up, she's sighted; escort in her wake.
Engines now in unison, a steady note they take.
Racing now to meet her, as children round her skirt,
Keeping watch on port and starboard; skippers on alert.
The navy now her escort; tugs to pave her way
With fire hoses raising a rainbow now of spray.

She cuts a monarch's figure, majestic, royal, proud.
Her pennant flying proudly, saluting Queen and crowd.
With grace she carries forward; flotilla follows through.
Seamanship and rank now command a better view.
The throbbing diesel engine and the coughing week end craft
Join ex-naval vessels and the rowboat trailing aft.
They've had their hour of glory, their patriotic say;
The spirit that was Dunkirk is with them still this day.
'Twas the Harbour Master's nightmare and the patriot's last dream;
They salute Britannia... as we salute our Queen.

Mistress Sea

I have no love, but that within my heart,
But never pity me.
Don't tell me what I lack; I lack not,
For faithful is my mistress sea.
I feel her freezing spray upon my face;
A thousand kisses raining.
A deck that strains and cries beneath my feet,
Yet thrives in her complaining.

I have no love to wait on winter shore;
Don't show concern.
I have no need of women's ways
Who promise much, then vengeful turn.
Old Neptune's nymphs have guided me
With cries of passion sending
My soul upon this journey rich
With pain and pleasure blending.

I have no love to give, I am not free;
I choose instead this life.
I'd rather ride each crested wave
Than gain a loveless wife.
Give me the wave that breaks my sleep
The storm that whips the ocean
And leave me be, bereft and free
Of any pained emotion.

Rounding the Horn

I'll tell you a story young nipper,
Of how we rounded The Horn;
How we steeple chased greybeards
That took old Neptune's form.
How we dared to fly top-sail
And carried our canvas well,
While clouds drove with fury of Hades
And the sea could be likened to hell.
Our jib boom climbed to the heavens,
Then dropped from each mountainous sea,
While the storm screamed satanic derision
And the devil, he screamed at me.
Our vessel cracked on through that snorter,
But we rounded The Horn without cost,
For although we suffered fair damage,
No men were injured or lost.
So I've told you a tale young nipper;
In Portsmouth I've bent your ear,
Reliving the glories of sail
While taking my baccy and beer.

Rat Catcher

I never asked to go to sea
For water I detest.
Not chosen for my company,
But the job I do the best.
I'm black and white and cunning
And move as fast as light.
My claws are sharp as razors;
Teeth strong enough to bite.
I am afraid of nothing,
Not man, nor beast or flea,
So heaven help the vermin
That takes a ride on me!
Although I wear no collar
Around my feline throat,
My eyes shine forth like buttons
Upon the captain's coat.
Then when I choose purr-fection
I groom myself to shine,
I wait beside the captain's chair
Until it's time to dine.
I purr and sidle slowly
And I will patient be
And when he drops a tit-bit
I take it for my tea.
But don't mistake my motive
And never call me tame,
For I am cruel by nature;
That's how I play the game.
I have no time to waste now;
It's time to catch a rat,
For that's the occupation of
This arrogant ship's cat.

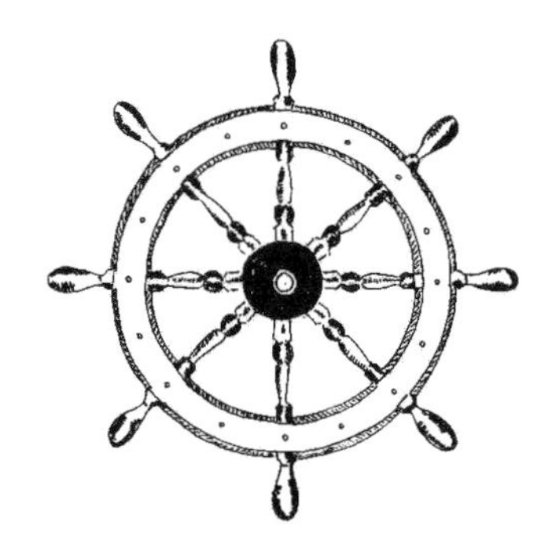

Safe Watch

There is one who travels with you,
Comes aboard to join your crew;
Stands aside through preparation
Watching everything you do.
Plots the course upon the table,
Reads the weather from the skies;
Joins the hand upon the wheel,
Being ears as well as eyes.
He will silently keep vigil,
Stand unseen upon the prow;
Answer prayers for your safe journey
As white waves wash the bow.
When you return to home port
And the harbour mouth yawns wide,
Praise the One who travelled with you;
For your God stood by your side.

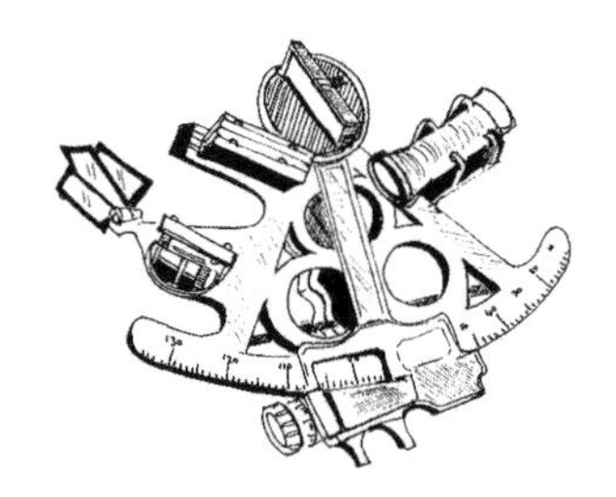

Line of Defence

Shaped like a diamond
Set in the sea,
More precious than any
Defences could be.
A garrisoned island
Shadowed your shore,
Protecting Old Portsmouth,
Southampton and more.
Lord Palmerston built
His forts in defence
Of the realm and the country
At costly expense.
The island strategically
Placed where it stands,
Gave natural protection
From enemy hands.
The risk of invasion
Is over at last,
Now your neighbourly island
Sleeps in your past.
But she is important
So value her do…
She keeps off the wind
And gives you your view!

Courageous Jim

Little Jim went off to sea,
Younger than his years;
It seemed he was an anxious lad,
Filled with child-like fears.
He packed the tackle he would need,
Though luxury was spare.
The only keepsake in his kit
Was Gran's red underwear!

Life aboard the ship was hell;
Jim wasn't worth his salt.
He worked as hard as any man,
So was it Jimmy's fault?
He didn't want to go to sea,
He really missed his Gran.
She loved him well from babe to boy,
Though soon he'd be a man.

Portsmouth Hard lay in their wake,
Departing seas ran fair.
They ran along the Cornish coast
And met their ill-fate there.
The storm whipped up a violent sea;
The crew screamed in alarm
And when the hull was torn on rocks,
Only Jim kept calm.

The rescuers could find no trace;
No salvage on the shore,
But as they searched beyond
the point,
The strangest sight they saw.
Above the water, calm by now,

A mizzen mast was rising
And tied by Gran's pink ribbon
Was something quite surprising!

The Cornish men in unison
Called to others there,
'By God we can not see the ship...
But look; red underwear!'
'Underwear,' the shout went up,
'How did that appear?'
Jim's weakened voice croaked, 'Under where?
No, we are under here!'

Ten men including Jim were saved,
Pulled from the cabin's grave
And Jim received a medal
For being bold and brave.
His fellow men were proud of Jim;
He had the wit to dare.
He couldn't fly the flag that night...
But he raised Gran's underwear!

No hidden agenda in this poem, just a laugh

The prison hulk York, Portsmouth

On May 13th 1787 eleven ships sailed as the First Fleet from Portsmouth to Botany Bay. This action was undertaken to relieve the overcrowding in British prisons, but also began the colonization of Australia by the British. Many minor crimes were punishable by transportation, including theft, even if it was undertaken for survival. Prisoners were accommodated on the prison hulks before beginning their epic journey. For many it was to be their last.

Some 736 convicts were eventually landed at Sydney Cove after horrendous conditions at sea. It took nine months to complete the voyage. This poem was written as a testament to the social history between our two countries and the population involved.

Bound for Botany Bay

Load her to the gun alls,
This ain't no Noah's Ark;
You're going on a journey
Cross the ocean, cruel and dark.

You don't deserve no quarter,
'Cause you're vile and mean as muck.
You should be hung on gallows;
That's your deserving luck.

You'll journey with the First Fleet,
To life on foreign ground.
You've languished on the prison ships,
Now you're Australia bound.

Your sentence, transportation;
New life, New World, new pain.
Don't get too high and mighty,
You won't see home again!

You won't look none too healthy
After months cooped up on board.

Best pray now to the devil...
Ain't no saving by the Lord.

You'll live in doubtless squalor
That harbours all disease.
Best knuckle down 'me hearties'
To life upon the seas.

We'll head for southern oceans;
Bound for Botany Bay.
It's there you'll have to settle
For it's there you'll have to stay!

'Tis time to slam the hatches,
You've wept your last goodbyes
To folk and to Old Portsmouth
And homely northern skies.

The entrance to Portsmouth harbour

At the entrance to Portsmouth Harbour stands The Round Tower and the defences known locally as The Hot Walls. These fortifications along the shore have been the watch-point of a nation through generations. How many matelot wives, girlfriends and families have stood in all weathers to wave off and to wave back their loved ones?

The story does not end in history; more recently we have viewed the Falkland Fleet, the *Ark Royal* outward bound for the Gulf conflict, the return and final departure of *H.M.Y. Britannia*. The list is endless and a book could be written from this view point alone.

Forgive me if I have written more than one 'leaving' poem. Stand on the beach below The Hot Walls any day and you will stand with others.

Preparing to Sail

There are rumours that the bum boats
Are starting to withdraw.
The traders and the women
Have been ordered back to shore.
For the fleet is making ready,
It will sail this winter's morn;
The Mother Bank is stirring
As seagulls fly at dawn.
By The Hot Walls crowds are swelling;
Wives and mothers on the beach,
Lasses staring seaward
With arms now out of reach
Of loved ones who are leaving,
Of the boys and of the men,
Knowing not when they will see them
Nor hold them once again.
The yards are raised and ready
And the canvas set to fall,
Now the Shanty man is calling,
Uniting one and all.

The crew is called to station
And the capstan bars are shipped,
While nippers go about the task
Of getting cable nipped.
The order has been given,
'Cable up and down'.
The anchor's raised from mooring bed;

The ship stands free of ground.
The sails are dropped at one command,
The canvas fill and crack.
The senses lift and hearts resign;
There'll be no turning back.
The crowd upon the shoreline pause
United as they stand,
Each utter up a silent prayer
For ships, now fully manned.
Then silent as a moving cloud
The Fleet is on its way,
Onward through St. Helens Roads;
Horizon claims the day.

The Leaving Tide

Now daylight touched the windowsill
Of Keppel's Head,
While folk of every decent class
Slept still in bed.
Yet within the street below
The throbbing had begun
With life, to call the day its own
And greet the morning sun.
A growing spill of people
Thronged within the street.
In one advancing hour
Folk jostled there to meet
The working wench, the Padre,
He hawker with his ware;
Their voices rising loudly;
Excitement filled the air.
In the city's distance
The clock struck of its chime,
While ladies and their gentlemen
From it took their time.
They dressed in finest feathers
And tunics brightly dyed
For this great occasion,
'The leaving on the tide'.

The dawn turned from its rosy light
In to the day anew.
With every inch of rising tide
A great excitement grew.
Matelots and their officers,
Whores of ample size;
Children and their kinsfolk
Said their fond goodbyes.
Now the vessels lifted gently,
At their moorings tried to pull.

On shore the mood was quickening;
The tide was rising full.
Midst the smell of thronging people,
Perfume and rough spilt ale
Came the order and the urgency;
The fleet was set to sail.
The boats pulled from the harbour,
While the landlord supped his beer,
For the Fleet and its departure
Takes his custom for the year.
Said the old salt to the nipper
Who was keen to go to sea,
'Listen and respect her son,
She'll make a man of thee!'

The end of Broad Street, Old Portsmouth

Outward Bound

The call has come that takes me now to sea.
The tide is full and so it calls to me.
My ship lies ready, restless to be gone
And I belong to her, yes I belong.

Provisions stowed and company complete.
There's promise of another land; new folk to meet.
Yet all I leave behind I'll not forget…
And yet my dearest love and yet.

The sea is calling me, it knows my name.
It's in my blood; it beats through every vein.
I can't ignore my passion's rising tide,
Though I must leave my bride; my bride.

The thronging crowd has gathered; she is there.
One longing look, I know her heart will tear
And yet already I'm away, I'm free.
Will Penny wait and wait for me?

The Parting

Tender are my feelings, aching is my heart,
For my ship lies ready, soon now to depart
And you my love are standing, a silhouette in space,
Brave and solitary, with quietness and grace.
Now the tide is rising and so we pull away
And yet my mind is bursting with all I want to say.
How I want to tell you, before my words are lost
In the wind of parting, on the waves so tossed.
Did I tell you darling, what you mean to me
How you bring me comfort, waiting patiently?
Did I say I love you? I will one day at length.
You are my companion, my love, my life my strength.
The tragedy of parting is loves unspoken word,
For it was left unuttered and now arrives unheard.
I watch for you to wave to me; I earnestly wave back,
For love does not diminish by the words I lack.

Farewell from the Round Tower

Johnny Leaves Me

Johnny leaves me now,
His vessel keen to haul
Her anchor from the mooring bed;
The mighty oceans call
And so away his figure
To join those chosen men.
His spirit left me long ago,
I don't remember when.
He told me how he loved me,
On the day that we were wed,
That he'd never take another
To our marriage bed.
So true those words, but worthless,
'Tis I who must stand back,
Though his mistress wears no petticoat
Or the bonnet that I lack.
She wears the darkest wardrobe,
Flecked with wind whipped white,
Though she becalms my fella,
When her mood is light.

For when she calls, he'll follow;
Follow to the sea.
'Tis if at night she whispers,
'Johnny come to me.'
Johnny leaves me now, a kiss and then away
And I will lie awake this night
In our bed and pray
That he will safe return to me,
His lust and urge well spent;
For he said he had a mistress
And I knew what Johnny meant!

Heave Away

Heave away lads and we'll be home
To Pompey; lady fair.
Soon to set our anchor down;
There'll be a welcome there.

Soon now lads we'll be ashore
And maiden's skirts will fly.
Soon our tankards brimming full;
We'll drink the taverns dry.

Soon now lads, so heave away;
Hear the topsail fill.
Soon to sight the harbour light...
Heave together still.

Soon now lads, first sight of home;
The smell of England's shore
And waiting by the Sally Port,
The lass who I adore.

So heave away my lads, don't let
The rhythm break or fall,
For Pompey calls her sailors home;
She calls them, one and all.

Homeward Bound

They cheered when we left Portsmouth
To serve our country well,
Achieving naval victory,
Though many seamen fell.
Although our ship is damaged,
Still proud and straight she sails,
For she took on the onslaught
Of canon and the gales.
We may be short of rations
And little left of beer;
Our weakened ship is homeward bound
And we have naught to fear.
Land will soon be sighted
And we shall smell the coast
And every man shall think again
Of those they love the most.
Gulls fly out to greet us;
We'll soon in Portsmouth be,
For like a faithful mistress
She calls us home from sea.

On the beach by the Round Tower

Awaiting News

The flame burns low, wax splutters;
I will replace anew
The candle in the window,
With hopes of you.

The alley's dark and cobbled;
The night is drawing late,
Yet by my sill I'm waiting
To know your fate.

They say the Fleet sails homeward,
But rumour's flying rife;
Perhaps already widowed,
This restless, watchful wife.

I knew you'd fought in battle,
Yet I heard little more.
I can not sleep or settle
Until I know for sure.

Pray God you'll come home safely;
That you are still alive.
How could we live without you?
How could we both survive?

Our child now is cradled
And suckles to my breast.
Until you stand beside us
We'll have little rest.

The morning breeze now catches
The tired candle's flame;
Is it imagination
Or did I hear my name?

I search the silent alley
With eyes brimmed full with tears,
For there, out of the shadows
My darling Tom appears.

My Dad

'He won't be home today son,'
That's what my Ma told me.
I listen for the gate to swing…
He'll come, eventually.

I walked with him that morning
He left to catch the train.
I was the last to see him,
But I know I will again.

Sometimes I remember
The things he used to say.
I'd like to grow up quickly
And be like him one day.

I try hard to imagine
His voice, his laugh, his hair.
I'm trying to catch shadows,
For I know he isn't there.

'Lost at sea,' Ma told me
And that I mustn't cry.
I know my Dad's a hero
And heroes do not die.

Sometimes I hear his footstep;
I talk to him in sleep.
But it will be our secret
For she'll never see me weep.

RESTAURANT
QUEENS HEAD
FRANK SULLIVAN
THE OLD LONDON
D95

H.M.S. WARRIOR

Whore's Cry

There'll be trade tonight my loverlies;
The Fleet is back in town.
Pennies for the table;
We'll bite the King's own crown.
Laughter in the alleys;
Shadows chasing light.
Best wear your gayest camisole;
You won't get sleep tonight!

Fleet's Return

Wearily we scan the clear horizon,
Dazzled by the glinting sunlit sea.
Taunted by the lack of wind to take us
Home to port, where we are bound to be.
Months have passed since we weighed anchor,
Having kissed the lasses well, who begged us stay.
Streets were full of love and lust and liquor,
While a mother choked a tear and turned away.

As we go about our duties so we ponder,
For menial tasks will cause a mind to drift.
Does Pa still spit and chew tobacco
At the end of every Dockyard shift?
Does darling Jenny carry now my child?
Something in me stirs upon the thought,
For life and love won't stop on parting;
I remember now the joy my Jenny brought.

Every man and boy who breathes amongst us,
Who fought and nearly died as numbered crew,
Will hold his eyes and heart fast forward
In hopes to catch horizon's changing view.
Soon will the cry go up; land will be sighted.
The straightened line into a serpent grow.
The land itself shall rise before us
And we shall see the land we love and know.

Now at last the wind begins to strengthen,
Our sails crack and billow to its call
And every man intent upon their duty,
Like harnessed horses heave to give their all.

'Land Ahoy', calls clearly from the crows nest.
We work not now as single men,
But straining in reply to urge us homeward;
We'll take no rest till we are home again.

We enter now the mooring channel,
To anchor with the British Fleet.
Time at last to man the cutters,
Our term at sea is now complete.
We burst upon the shore in expectation,
Along The Hard to spend the well earned crown;
But me? This day I hurry home to Jenny,
With beating heart and ribbons for her gown.

A Cutter returns

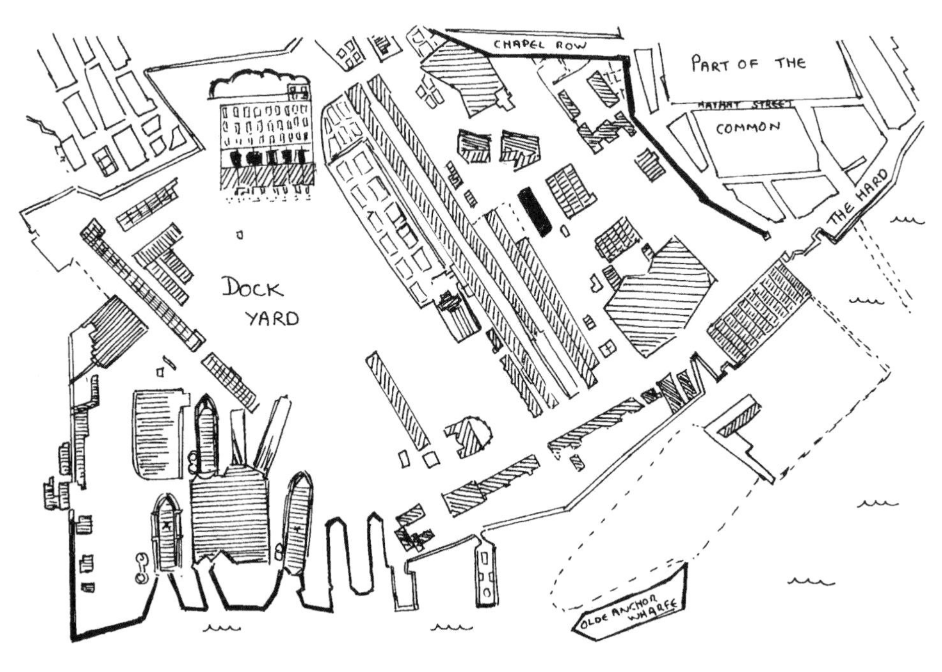

Portsmouth Royal Dockyard at the time

Jack Hill, alias Aitkins, a Scot by birth and a painter by trade was eventually caught, tried and punished for his heinous crime of treason. His sympathies lay with America at this time and his aim was to bring down Britain by firing the Dockyards of Portsmouth and Plymouth. Successful in his attempt at firing Portsmouth Royal Dockyard and the all important Rope House, his freedom was short lived.

His punishment on March 10th 1777 was by hanging from the mast of the Arethusa, which had been re-erected at The Main Gate of the Dockyard. The now unemployed rope makers were given their revenge. Jack's body was tarred and remained on view long after his crime, before eventually being laid to rest.

Visiting Americans find it a fascinating story, though in jest their loyalty is divided.

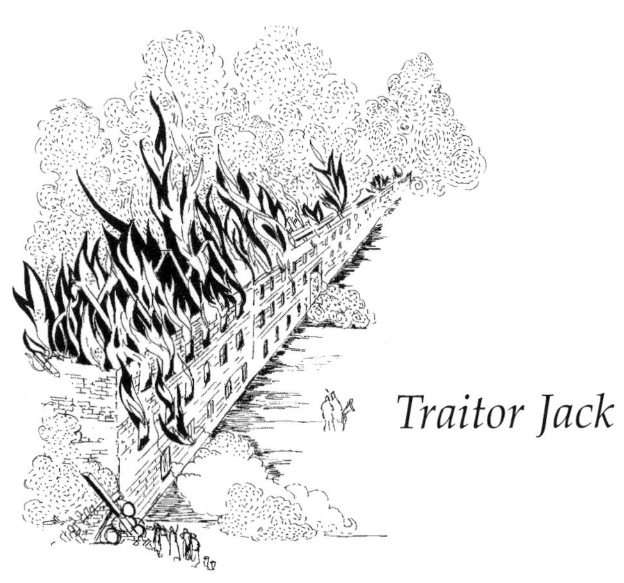

Traitor Jack

There's a story for the telling
Of Jack, the painter bold,
Loyal to America,
Though a Scotsman we are told.
Jack's thoughts were dark with arson;
Sabotage his game.
He planned with skill and cunning
To set the Yard aflame.
Employed within the Dockyard
He assumed a painter's trade.
In the privacy of lodgings
Incendiaries he made.
One night the Dockyard rope-house
Fired to the sky;
Our warships without rigging
Were forced in port to lie.
Jack looked that night from Portsdown;
Success stood by his side.
He'd fired The Royal Dockyard...
But it was hard to hide.
Caught, tried and convicted,
His debt must now be paid
By punishment of hanging;
An example to be made.

They pulled him on the tumbrel
To the Yard from Portsmouth gaol,
To a mizzen mast erected
With hanging rope, not sail.
Rope makers given vengeance
Hauled the villain high,
So as his hours were numbered
He looked down from the sky
And saw the burnt out Rope-house
From his gallows by the gate
And heard the angry voices
And felt their burning hate.
Jack hung there for an hour,
Upon that rope he died.
Then tarred at Pitchhouse Jetty;
A decent fate denied.
At Blockhouse Point they set him,
Caged and in full view,
A warning that this sentence
Could be carried through.
Jack became a relic
And local lads would jeer;
A target for ridicule
Whenever they passed near.
Till one night they took him
Drinking for a jest;
When at last recovered
Jack was laid to rest.

Cross Street, Portsea

The social history of life in the city of Portsmouth in the 18th and 19th century was one of poverty and hardship. The tightly packed housing and poorly lit alleys in the poorer areas bred disease and often circumstances were worsened by fluctuating employment within large families. Child mortality was high and much was against them. However it must be remembered that family life was close and strictly disciplined. The family was important and they made the best of 'their lot'. Later much was done to improve the social structure within the city.

A great deal has been written on this subject but my poetry in this selection has been inspired by the overall love and commitment. There was a freedom to enjoy simple pleasures in childhood games that we can now days only envy!

Favoured Joe

He sleeps; the candle gutters,
He lies still on my arm.
I took him to my bed for work,
Yet now in sleep he's calm.
The urgency has left him,
Aye and the sights he saw.
For Joe, my favoured matelot
Came straight to me from war.

He shouts down in the alley,
'Where's Mol, my heart's desire?'
With coins upon the table,
He knows I am for hire
And yet my heart beat swiftly
As he tripped the landing stair.
I knew he'd come a calling;
He knew that I'd be there.

Law, I didn't care his status,
Or the roughness of his hands
As I held him to my bosom;
For Molly understands.
Soon he'll stir and leave me,
Looking back not at my door,
But coins burn in his pocket;
Joe will be back, for sure.

Our Sal

The scream was high, the muffled cry
Was heard in Blossom Alley.
Exhausted sigh, would our Mom die
Giving birth to Sally?
We heard her fight throughout the night,
Though we kept out the way.
In early morn our Sal was born;
We heard Ma Johnson pray.
The door ajar, 'ah, there you are;
Come look your sister's sleeping.'
Yet all the while Mom tried to smile
I saw that she'd been weeping.
We entered three, Pat, John and me
While Tom was fetching water.
As fate would be, Dad was at sea;
He never saw his daughter.
The months have passed; now at last
The sun shines through our alley.
We would be five, were she alive,
But Jesus wanted Sally.

Blossom Alley, Portsea

The Mudlarks

It's slimy, it's slippy and ever so sticky.
It's sloppy and sucks at your toes
And yet it's exciting and very inviting,
But don't yer get none on yer clothes.

It's mucky and mushy and ever so muddy,
But cakes on yer face when it dries.
Getting an earful is vergin' on tearful
And stings when it gets in yer eyes.

We're happy and hopeful and not very heedful;
We're down on The Hard at low tide,
Ducking and diving, no thought of surviving;
Our clothes piled up on the side.

A penny comes pitching as Thomas is hitching
His pants, sucked by mud from his waist.
With joy Joe is whooping, laughing and scooping
The coin through his fingers in haste.

'Throw us another for my little brother,'
Frank yells to the folk passing by.
Tossed in an inkling the penny starts sinking
And is lost in the wink of an eye.

The tide now is rising and it's not surprising
Our mud larking game is now through.
Time now for scrubbing, best now to get rubbing;
Don't let any mud stick to you.

Our mother's inspection, without an exception
Is close, so it's best to beware.
Check trousers and shirt for the least sign of dirt
And make sure there's no mud in your hair.

The Hard at low water

Dockyard Errand

'Molly fly, the bell is ringing,
Leave the washing dear.
Take your Dad his dinner,
His bowl and jug of beer.'

Molly stopped what she was doing;
Dried her hands and smiled,
Eager now to run her errand.
'Hurry do now child!'

She took the jug from her mother
And the cloth wrapped bowl.
Smiling as she skipped the doorstep.
'On your way now Mol.'

Out the yard and down the alley,
Half a mile or more.
Keen to see her working father
At the Dockyard store.

Meeting friends and other children;
Scared of being late.
Soon our Molly, fairly breathless
Reached the Dockyard gate.

Clutching tight her father's dinner
Molly joined the crowd
Thronging through the Naval Dockyard;
Busy, noisy, loud.

Soon she found her hungry father;
Handed him the jug.
He took the beer and bowl of dinner,
Giving her a hug.

Mol sat down beside her father,
Watching as he ate.
Until he finished every morsel
She would sit and wait.

When her Dad had finished eating,
Hands like plates of meat
Patted Molly on her shoulders,
'That went down a treat.'

He stood; his dinner break was over.
Looking down he smiled.
He gave Mol back the empty bowl
And bent to kiss his child.

Mol left the Yard and walked The Hard;
Her heart and load were light,
For soon the Dockyard bell would send
Her father home that night.

The Main Gate Portsmouth Dockyard

Up to the twentieth century family members were allowed within the Dockyard to take in meals for the workers.

For the Love of Aunt Jessie

She passes me each day, on duty at the gate.
I'd set my watch by her, she's never late.
I do not know her well, it's not my place;
A comely lass, but fair of face.
She carries on her arm a basket full of scraps,
Brought from her own table, or treat perhaps.
Not for me you understand; oh no, not that!
She's come to feed the strays and any Dockyard cat.
They wait for her you know; it's really weird.
You don't see none of them till she's appeared.
The ginger, the tabby and tortoiseshell cross
All take their cue from Blackie, the boss.
They must be watching, eyes wide and alert.
They hear her step and rustle of skirt.
She makes for her station; the same every day.
I'd give her a medal if I had my way.
She'll open the basket, then stop to call

And cats come arunning, like kids out of school.
She places out dishes and tries to be fair,
Though often a moggie gets more than its share.
They have their order, from timid to mean.
The scraps are soon eaten and plates are licked clean.
She treats them as children; an auntie for sure
And when it is finished, she tells them,'No more.'
She'll be here at Christmas, come rain or come sleet,
Never forgetting that cats have to eat.
Without her devotion they wouldn't survive,
Because she is caring they're fed and they thrive.
I take my cap off to ladies like her,
Whose heart has been softened by whiskers and fur.

There really was an Aunt Jessie and many more women who took it on themselves to care for the strays at the Dockyard.

The ancestors of some of these moggies would probably have had stories to tell about Nelson. What greater pedigree than that?

'The Sentinel' was inspired by The Fort Cumberland Guard Society, a re-enactment group founded in 1965 by local enthusiasts.

The Cumberland Guard takes its name from the bastion fortress on the Eastney peninsula and models itself on the Royal Marine Light Infantry of 1830. The original Fort Cumberland was built in 1746 as part of the Duke of Richmond's scheme to fortify the coast.

The Sentinel

Be proud, they said, when country calls
And now I stand to guard these walls.
Marching now to silent beat,
Aware of naught but aching feet.
My hand is stiff, my rifle sleeps
As morning from its slumber creeps.
I march as clockwork painted toy
I well remember as a boy.
Yet now the battle that I fight
Is boredom born of left and right.
Of steps repeat and turns rehearsed,
Oh how my dreary watch is cursed
By furrowed walk as farmer's plough.
Where sounds the call to battle now?
To glory sails the lads I knew,
Yet as a sentinel I view
Their wave, their wake, their energy;
Their call to England's victory.
Though few will ever bless my name,
I serve my country just the same,
For while I guard Old Portsmouth's shore
I'll keep the wolf outside the door.
Monotony shall bring reward
And valour to my sleeping sword.

Harbour fortifications

The Local Look

There's a certain look that's common to each face.
It's one that even time can not erase.
It tells you not of present, lighter life,
But haunting hardship, hurt and strife.
An imprint from another age; a social stamp,
When women waited on The Hard by light of lamp.
Who, with their children gathered round their knees
Prayed for safe return of men folk from the seas.
Then again through war and bombing driven
From their homes, to share the little they'd been given.
How they clung together, disregarding all they lacked
Codes of life and loyalty; the family life intact.
Hardship was the thread that ran the weave
Of life and death, allowing time to grieve
And now the past has lost its valued place,
Yet look with care and wisdom at each face
Each line of hardship etched in life soon dies
Yet still the local look is read behind their eyes.

The Beach

Don't remember me for how I died,
Nor those who stood beside my name and cried.
Remember me as youth in sunlight falling,
Before the days of battle calling.
Remember still my laugh and carefree smile
Before I ran that screaming mile.
Hear me again upon your listening ear,
Whispered words in essence to appear
And stand amongst the shadows of the beach,
Knowing I am here, though out of reach.
I shall not haunt your day, nor set
The seal of sadness on the scene;
Nor have I need of pastures green,
For I am free;
Why can't you see…
Forever I am living.

This poem has been included as a mark of respect to all those involved in the D-Day Landings and the preparations, much of which took place along the South coast of England.

Dawn Horizon

Grey dawn from darkest night
And sea that's greyer still
Demands no more or less
Than Neptune's will
That troughs and swells,
Though silent as the grave,
Commanded by the surging force
Within each wave.

First flush of lightened dark;
Advancing day,
Diminishing the night,
Sent on her way.
A line defines
And cuts the scene in two,
As sea and sky divide at last
As light breaks through.

Cold watch, now energy and thought
Once side by side
Play tricks and wish in warmth
And safety to reside.
Eyes scan horizon grey
And sky of silver slate,
While children sleep at home
Unaware of father's fate.

Watch called; another day
As duty's sentinel must stand.
Yet straight will be that line,
No sight or thought of land.
Monotonous and menacing,
Horizon's circle calls.
Will life or death materialize
Before new darkness falls?

This emotive poem was written as a tribute to the men who served on the Atlantic convoys of the two world wars. Such films like The Cruel Sea were my inspiration. Gripping the armchair in front of the black and white television, wondering if the boys would come home. Many didn't; this is for them.

H.M.Sm. *Swordfish* sailed from Gosport on November 7th 1940, to commence war patrol off Brest, France. In 1983 Island marine archaeologist Martin Woodward discovered the wreck south of St Catherine's Point, off the Isle of Wight. The mystery of her loss, always presumed to be off of the French coast, was solved. She had hit a mine a few hours out of home port while making a dive, with the loss of all forty of her crew. Those who may have escaped the submarine would have perished in the freezing water.

The illustration shows her before passing through the Anti Submarine boom between Horse Sand Fort and Nettlestone Point.

The poem was inspired by the tragedy of her crew and their families.

Deep Secret

She sailed from Gosport during the war,
Nobody guessing what was in store.
Ordered off Brest to take up patrol,
She never took on her dutiful role.

Assumed by her silence that she had been lost;
Mined off of France and suffered full cost.
On November 7th this story should end,
But on future fate the truth would depend.

The sea took her secret; locked in the deep,
Allowing the truth of the tragedy sleep.
She gave no inkling of what was below;
Evidence held that no one could know.

The sea whispered secrets no one would hear,
Until at last, in the forty third year
The wreck of The *Swordfish* came then to light,
She'd been blasted, destroyed off the Isle of Wight.

Loved ones entombed for so many years,
In sight of home, it now appears.
Our sea served them well, protecting their grave
Now they're at peace, sub-mariners brave.

HMSm. Swordfish dressed overall

The Shipwright

Just an ordinary man upon the street,
No one special, though someone you may meet.
Yet ask him of his work one passing day,
'Shipwright in the Yard,' he's bound to say.
Though body slightly bent, your eye is held;
Something in his manner holds you now, compelled
To ask of him and hear his shipwright's tale,
Though he never worked as some with ancient sail.
His past is bound by heritage and royal law,
Founded by the will for peace and strength of war.
So proud, this crafted man, of skills well taught,
He will recount experience his trade has brought.
Proud of the ships he built with muscle and with brain,
With sweat and danger too; 'gainst wind and rain.
The launching of each vessel made his spirit soar.
Alas now but a memory; alas no more.
He will recount with sentiment her shape divine,
Knowing every inch of her and every line.
For with such pride he'd touched her steel girth,
Knowing he was part of her, present at her birth.
Those days have long departed, as slips in silence stand.
It's hard for modern folk like us to understand,
But ask a Dockyard shipwright of the Navy and the sea
And he will say, 'To honour them, you must acknowledge me!'

H.M.S. Dreadnought

To serve a Dockyard apprenticeship in the 1950's would have taken a lad five years. This was a reduction from the seven years it took in earlier times. The time honoured skills of the shipwright have given way to modern materials and methods to match the new technology. In 1995 even the shipwright's title was changed to 'plate fabricator'.

The defence review of 1981 resulted in massive imminent redundancies within the Dockyard. On Friday April 2nd 1982 workers received notification of redundancy. 3750 jobs were threatened in the General Managers Department alone.

The decision was to be made between 10am and 11am on that day. The mood was one of impending gloom. Also on Friday April 2nd 1982 Argentina invaded The Falklands Islands.

The word came through,
'We are sending The Fleet south.'
The Dockyard workforce responded to the call,
'Ships must sail Monday'.

Closure

My saddened eyes can see no more
The rush of men from slip and store;
The tolling bell that sent men home
Now as an artifact is known.
Ears can not hear the union shout.
No whistling men; no Tom about.
No cycle bells, or ribald jeer,
For silence drops on listening ear.
No working mass in gathered strength
To hear the arguments at length.
Struck as a tree, not one by one,
But felled as wood when work was done.
They talk of sailors lost at sea,
Who lived and died heroically.
They honour soldiers from the war
Yet on our men they closed the door.
They took their packets, their last wage,
While politicians turned the page.
The book was closed but will remain
An epitaph to every name.

The workforce leaving through Unicorn Gate

A Way of Life

Have you ever walked the Dockyard?
Have you stood where Nelson fell?
Well you don't know the half of it,
That much I can tell.
I bet you haven't wondered
As you've queued outside the Gate,
'Bout the families who've been raised there,
'Bout their lives as well as fate?
You have to walk each alley
And leave the milling crowd
To appreciate the Dockyard
That has made Old Portsmouth proud.
There are stories I could tell you
'Bout officers and crew;
Of alley cats and Admirals,
For I have known a few.
There are names that conjure magic
And buildings by the score;
Passages for people who
Don't pass this way no more.
My role was treating sailors;
I signed some to the knife.

Within the Dockyard

Short Row, Portsmouth Naval Base

I took it all for granted,
It was my way of life.
There were parties after midnight
And commodores for tea;
Gardeners for gardening
And Dockyard trips for free.
So don't forget The Dockyard
At the setting of the sun.
Of the folk who lived there,
I was only one.

This poem was written in memory of
Surgeon Commander P. M. Browne RN (Rtd)
1923-2003

Cathedral Store

If the world had ever lost me,
I would have turned the key
Then entered this old storehouse
And found tranquility.

A cathedral for my spirit;
This quiet, empty place,
With soft and slanting sunlight
That gives cold shadows chase.

Nothing quite specific
Can I bring to mind,
Yet peace is all around me;
Within as well, I find.

I climb forbidden stairways,
For public, out of bound
And though no recollection
I feel on common ground.

I stand on wooden flooring,
Planked from ships of old.
This silent, giant storehouse
Holds stories still untold.

The air rests thick around me
As dust upon the floor,
While watching eyes watch over
Their workplace evermore.

I listen to the timbers
That rise to rafted roof.
They whisper of their industry
With unreported truth.

These walls of brick once painted,
Now crumble, red in dust.
The air is still and dry now;
No smell of damp or must.

'Tis if these halls are waiting
For some official hand
To honour recognition
Of where and why they stand.

One day this place will echo
With population's voice.
The memories then captured
And tamed for public choice.

But now it's my cathedral;
The past lies still and thick.
History's absorbed in
Each wall, each plank, each brick.

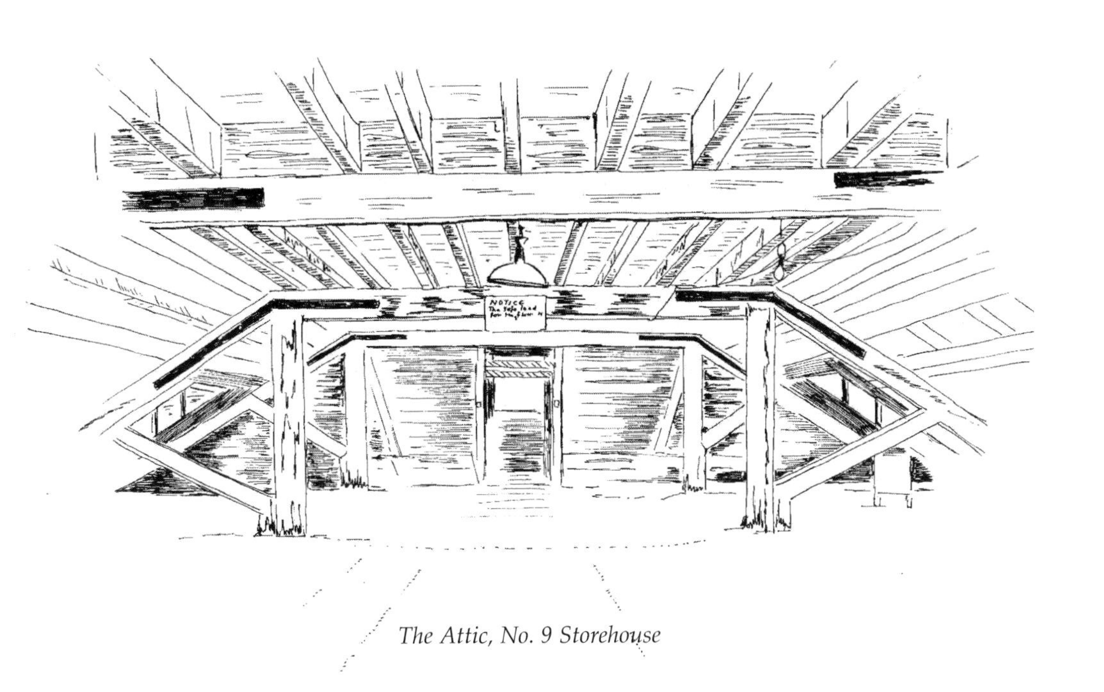

The Attic, No. 9 Storehouse

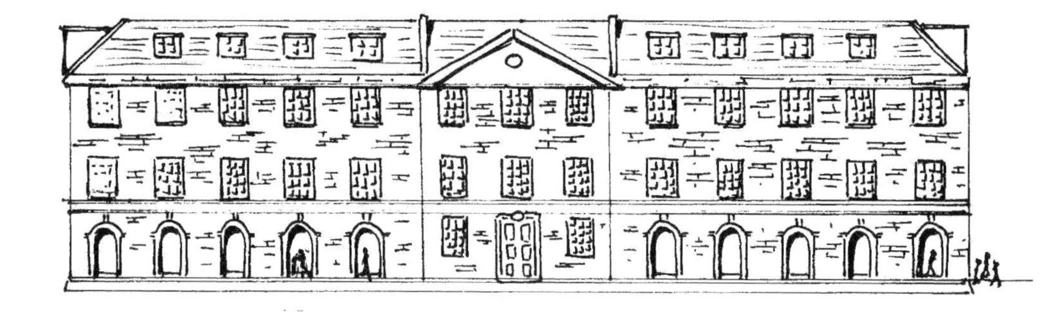

No 9 Storehouse

The previous poem was written during a privileged visit to the great Georgian Storehouses at Portsmouth Historic Dockyard. The upper storey of No 9 Storehouse, built as its neighbours in red brick and reused ships timbers is now redundant of its previous usage and lies empty, away from public scrutiny. Standing in this cathedral-like attic it was easy to envisage the immense volume of stores and equipment once held in these huge storehouses.

The Heritage Area of the Royal Dockyard is educational and open for the enjoyment of the public who come to visit the great ships and The Naval Museum, along with many of the exhibitions. The area allows scope for future projects and festivals. Harbour trips enable the public to view the modern Royal Navy and her visitors at anchor. The past and present co-habit comfortably, as does fact and creative explanation.

The School Outing

We went to Portsmouth Dockyard,
My friend Bill Bates and me
And thirty other school friends;
Did teacher get in free?
We went aboard The *Warrior*,
The steel clad man-of-war
And every deck we went on
I wanted to explore.

We went to see The *Mary Rose*;
She made an awesome view.
I saw her through a window
'Cause you couldn't get close to.
We saw the exhibitions
Behind The Dockyard walls;
The artifacts recovered
And all the shipwright's tools.

I liked The *Victory* the best;
I stood where Nelson fell,
But apart from the inscription
You really couldn't tell.
Bill Bates and Sylvia got caught
Behind the bulkhead snogging!
The guide said, 'Son, behave yourself.
You'll get a sailor's flogging!'

We saw an awful lot that day;
I spent my pocket money.
I'm sorry that it poured with rain…
I'll go back when it's sunny!

Volunteers

Unsung, part paid;
Volunteers self-made.
Keen eyed, strong hand;
Working well, jobs planned.
Old skills retaught;
Ideas rethought.
One aim, one dream;
Many men, one team.
Willing hearts, worthy cause;
Little praise, no applause.
Ringing out dirty rags;
Counting out naval flags.
Rubbing down, painting up;
Tea in mug, no cup.
Pumping out, turning rope;
Old boats, new hope.
Salvaging useful parts;
One dream, all hearts.
Workshop, little heat;
Pride in jobs, when complete.
Mast Pond, tidal draft;
Small boats, landing craft.
Damp feet, rolled sleeves;
One 'skip' who believes
All men have skill,
Eager hands, iron will.
Pull together, one rope;
Heritage, England's hope.
Volunteers stand tall,
All for one and one for all.

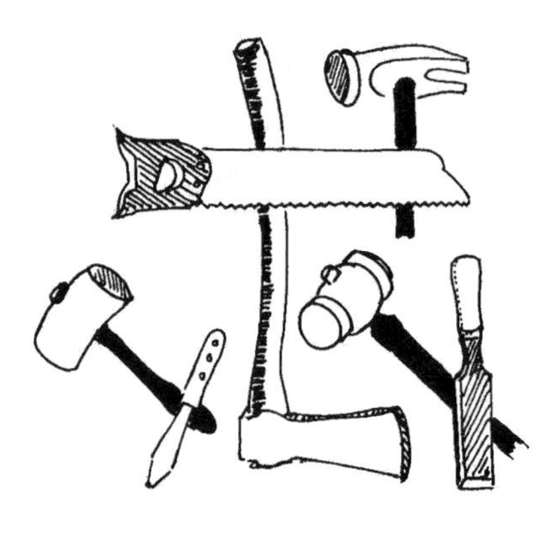

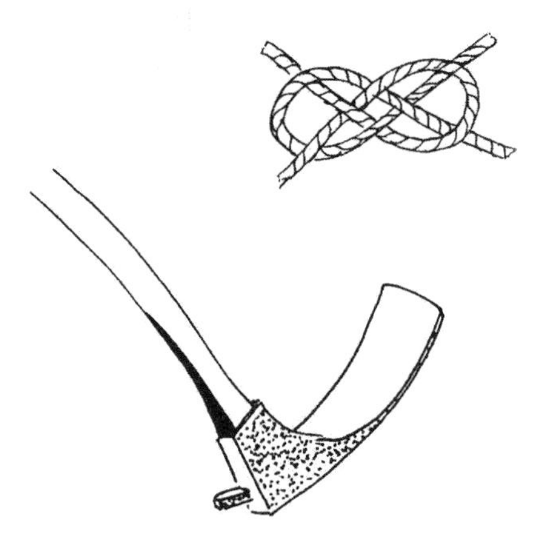

An enthusiastic group of volunteers at the Historic Dockyard at Portsmouth, under the guidance of Mr. Brian Patterson, Curator & Keeper of Historic Boats, maintain the collection and the equipment within the Heritage Area, using the Mast Pond and pontoon for mooring and display.

The Harbour Launch D49 and the Commander-in-Chief's Barge (The *Green Parrot*) have been restored and exceptionally maintained and are often seen on regular trips within and outside the harbour boundary taking their V.I.P. visitors out at the various festivals held throughout the year.

Without these volunteers many of the smaller boats would be lost in disrepair.

The Green Parrot

The Commander-in-Chief held official position,
His barge, The *Green Parrot* went with the commission.
On many occasion it must be known
She's carried the Monarch and heirs to the throne.
Built once for service for Navy and Queen,
Again in her glory *'The Parrot'* is seen.
Her livery painted in green of her class,
Her chrome painted dolphins polished like glass.
Her decks have been varnished, she's groomed for the course;
Less of a boat, more a thoroughbred horse.
Her lounges are ready, awaiting inspection,
Mahogany polished to see your reflection.
This forty five footer, an elegant craft,
Lovingly cared for from bow through to aft.

The Commander in Chief's Barge in 2004

She's still a fine lady, this C in C's barge
And governs respect from boats small and large.
Cared for and tended, maintained the year through,
By men who work hard as her volunteer crew.
Though not now in service, tradition's her name,
She'll pull at her moorings, her life to reclaim.
Time now to be out; It's time to make ready.
The skipper's aboard; the vessel holds steady.
He checks her position and calls on his crew;
Each at his station to follow on through.
Her engine is fired and soon she will be
Flying and famous, full throttle and free.

The Green Parrot outside Portsmouth Harbour

The Language of the Sea

I'm joining the crew of this vessel,
For a land-lubber it's quite a task,
For I understand very little
And I've oceans of questions to ask.

Is it a boat that I sail on,
Or a ship, or a launch, or a craft?
Is the bow of a ship at the sharp end?
Is the blunt end known as aft?

I'm told that the ship, that is female,
Is fickle and fine and runs free,
But you'll find if you disrespect her,
'Man overboard' means, 'in the sea.'

Now the ship; is it steered by the wheel
Or the helm on the bridge of the boat?
Is he the captain or skipper,
The man who keeps her afloat?

Then there's the port and the starboard;
My they don't talk my language at all.
I can't tell my left from my right hand,
Let alone the direction they call.

There's something I can't really fathom
When they measure the depth of the sea.
Why don't they tell me in inches
How close to the bottom we be?

And when we start to get speed up
They talk of knots to confuse.
Oh goodness my brain's really tangled;
I think it's all just a ruse.

The vitals are cooked in the galley,
But fenders protect the ship's side.
The don't take much notice of hours,
For time is dependant on tide.

There's talk of ladders and hatchways,
Of lockers and stowage below.
No mention of stairs nor of cupboards;
There really is too much to know.

If you think you're about to be sick then
The direction of wind you must check
And don't think of cleaning the floor 'cause
They'll sure make you scrub down the deck.

Oh I want to belay and make fast now,
Come ashore with my feet on dry land,
For I'll never be happy at sea when
They use language I can't understand!

The Harbour launch outing

Hearts Harbour

At first there were no lights upon life's sea,
The boat I sailed was in fact me.
The wind blew and currents ran.
The ocean deep filled life's earthly span.
Once anchor weighed the journey had begun.
My compass guide was both the stars and sun.
From these my soul would learn to recognize
And slowly they'd become my comfort and my eyes.

Every now and then emotions did becalm.
A sense of peace ensued, subsiding my alarm.
The waves and growing storm would whip the sea.
I was fearful then of what life asked of me
And yet my boat was safe and strong,
Though sea was often rough and journey long.
Oft I saw a shoreline upon horizon clear,
Despite the urgent longing, never to grow near.

Yet upon my journey I learnt many things;
How to sail my own craft, how my spirit sings.
How to pray when life blows up a storm,

To give up thanks for calmer seas and breezes warm.
How to tend the sails, taking up the slack.
Discovering my strength and things I lack.
Finding courage; learning how to stand
When my boat is rocking and life gets out of hand.

Now I see a land mass forming fast
And feel, very soon, that I'll be home at last.
To a familiar harbour my spirit calls its home,
Somewhere sure to moor my boat, safe from storm and foam.
So long upon life's seas I've fought my way,
I find it hard to realize that I'm allowed to stay
Safe within this shelter my heart has cried to find.
Life's sea gave me my wisdom and you my peace of mind.

Town Quay, Portsmouth

Conclusion

And as I rest my pen
Upon the page complete,
'Tis time for present
And the past to meet.
A portrait drawn
Of life no more
And yet my friend
Are you so very sure?
Take pause and scratch the surface
Of the life you lead
And know that it was history
That planted the first seed.

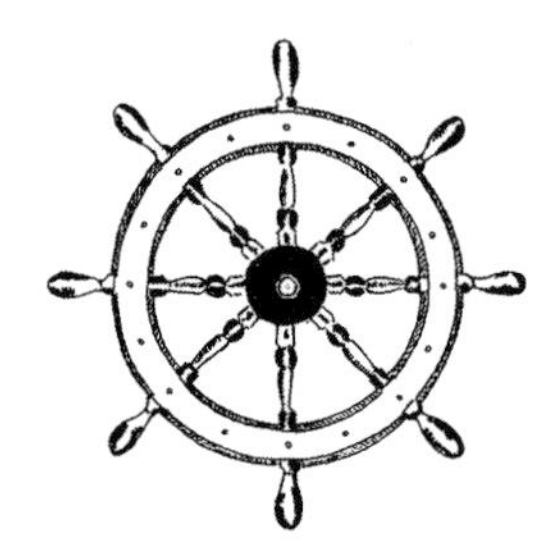

About the Author and Illustrator

Lynn New was born in Jersey and although she spent her childhood in Dunstable, she returned to the Channel Islands in 1971 to commence a nursing career. She moved to Guernsey and then to the Isle of Wight, which has been her home for over twenty years, proving that islands and the sea are very much part of her life. She would not want to move away from the coast and has happily accepted Portsmouth and its enthralling history, so close on her doorstep,as a large part of her recent life.

Lynn has written and illustrated six books, although Time and Tide is the first she has published herself. She is known for her highly illustrated anthologies which are published on the Island, but are sold nationally and internationally. She is a prolific writer and artist and her range extends to greeting cards and allied products and prints. Her thirst for new projects seems quite limitless, which is good news for anybody who is appreciative of her creative talent.